"So now I give him to the Lord. For his whole life he will be given over to the Lord."
1 Samuel 1:28 NIV

To Erik

SAMUEL
Judge and Prophet
Retold by Anne deGraaf
Illustrated by José Pérez Montero
© Copyright 1991 by Scandinavia Publishing House
Nørregade 32, DK-1165 Copenhagen K

English-language edition published through
special arrangement with Scandinavia by
Wm. B. Eerdmans Publishing Co.,
255 Jefferson Ave. S.E., Grand Rapids, Michigan 49503
All rights reserved
Printed in Hong Kong

ISBN 0-8028-5037-5

SAMUEL
Judge and Prophet

Written by Anne de Graaf
Illustrated by José Pérez Montero

Eerdmans

God thinks children are extra special. He has a special place in His heart for children, no matter where they come from. Why is this? Because of the way children laugh. Because they believe when adults sometimes doubt. Because children trust what they hear.

Samuel was a little boy who trusted what he heard. When God spoke to Samuel, he believed. Samuel was extra special because even when he grew up, Samuel kept on listening to God.

The story of Samuel begins before he was born. It begins with his parents, Hannah and Elkanah. They wanted to have a baby very much. As the years went by, though, no baby came. So Elkanah married a second wife. Her name was Peninnah. Peninnah could have many children.

Because of this Peninnah was very mean to Hannah. "You're a useless wife! You can't even give Elkanah one baby!"

Hannah tried not to listen. She knew Elkanah loved her more than Peninnah. Elkanah's love made up for Peninnah's cruelty.

Every year Elkanah took his family to Shiloh. There they prayed to God. They thanked Him for all the good things He had given them.

During the feast in Shiloh Elkanah gave Hannah twice as much meat as Peninnah. Peninnah watched him do this. Worse than the meat, she saw the look of love on Elkanah's face. "He never looks at me that way," she thought jealously.

Peninnah waited until she was alone with Hannah. Then she flew at her in anger. "Who do you think you are? You're not so special! Just look at you! You're getting old, Hannah!"

Hannah knew what was coming. She covered her ears, but could not keep out Peninnah's screaming.

"Look at all my children! You don't have any! What will you do when you are really old? You won't have any children to care for you! Hannah, are you listening? Ha ha!" Peninnah laughed at Hannah.

Poor Hannah. She felt as if her heart were breaking. She ran away and cried. When Elkanah found her he guessed what had happened.

"Don't listen to Peninnah," he told her.

"Babies aren't so important. Look at the way I love you, Hannah. Isn't that better than ten sons?"

How could Hannah tell him what she felt? She thought, "Babies *are* important! My wanting a baby doesn't take away from my love for him. Even Elkanah doesn't know how I feel!"

Hannah burst into tears and turned away from Elkanah. She ran to the tent where they went to pray. Inside were the stone tablets with God's Ten Commandments written on them.

An old priest named Eli was in charge of this place of prayer at Shiloh. When he saw Hannah come running inside and fall on the ground, he did not know what to think.

Eli watched Hannah closely. Her lips were moving.

"O Lord," she whispered. "You know how much I want to have a baby. Please, Lord, please help me!" Hannah's tears fell onto the ground.

"Please God, if You were to give me a son, I would give him back to You. I promise. I would bring him back to Shiloh and let this priest bring him up. The boy would be Yours, please Lord!"

Eli had seen enough. The woman's eyes were red. She was mumbling to herself. "She must be drunk," he told himself. Eli had seen too many people come to Shiloh and do nothing but eat and drink. They often stumbled into the tent where Eli kept the Ten Commandments. It was his job to ask them to leave. "Only praying people should come here, not drunks like this woman," Eli sighed.

He pointed a finger at Hannah. "You there!" he called out. "I don't want drunks in here. Get out!"

Hannah looked up in surprise. "Oh, sir, I'm not drunk. My heart is broken. I'm pouring out my troubles to God."

Eli took a closer look at Hannah. He could see she was deeply upset. "Go in peace," he told her. "May the Lord bless you and give you what you have asked for."

Hannah thanked Eli for his blessing. As she walked away, she felt the weight of worry and shame lift. She did not know how, but she knew everything would be all right.

After this, whenever Peninnah teased Hannah, Hannah could ignore her. This was because Hannah knew God had heard her prayers.

It did not take long for Hannah to discover she was finally going to have a baby! Oh, that was a happy day for her and Elkanah. They prayed for their baby during the months he grew inside Hannah.

The day finally came when Hannah gave birth to a healthy little boy. "Samuel," she told Elkanah. "I want to call this baby Samuel, because that means 'God hears.' God heard my prayers and just look how much He has blessed us!"

Samuel was a special child from the moment he was born. He was the answer to their prayers. Hannah poured all her love into Samuel. She sang to him and cuddled with him.

Sometimes Peninnah still teased her, "I have many children and you only have one!"

But Hannah would say, "My son Samuel is worth more than all your children put together." Samuel was such a good boy. He could make both his mother and father laugh and smile.

As Samuel learned how to walk and talk, Hannah taught him games. She danced with her little boy until they both fell on the ground, dizzy and laughing.

"Oh Samuel, I love you so much." Hannah told him. "But God loves you even more." Samuel hugged his mother.

Samuel's mother did not forget her promise to God. She had trusted God to hear her prayers. She had promised to give her child back to God. She would trust God to take care of her son.

Many times Samuel's mother had told him, "The most important lesson you can learn is to trust and believe in God."

When Samuel was old enough to walk and talk and feed himself, his parents brought him to Shiloh. Samuel knew this meant he was a big boy. Only the big children went to Shiloh to pray.

His mother told him about an old man who lived there. "His name is Eli. Eli is a priest. He's going to take care of you. I will come and visit every year."

Samuel walked toward the tent with his mother. He tugged on her hand. "How long is a year?"

Before she could answer, though, they entered the tent. Samuel heard his mother say to an old man, "Eli, remember me? You blessed my prayers when I asked God for a baby. I promised this child to God. Now he is old enough for you to take care of him and teach him about God."

Eli bent down and held out his arms to Samuel. "Welcome, little friend," he said.

Samuel thought about how his parents had told him God would take care of him no matter where he was. Samuel let Eli hug him. When he turned around, his mother was gone. "I'm not afraid," he told himself. Samuel trusted his parents and he trusted the Lord.

13

During the years to come, Samuel saw his mother once a year. Each time she visited, she brought Samuel a new little robe.

Meanwhile, Eli taught Samuel about God's laws for His people, the Ten Commandments. He also taught Samuel about prayer.

"Prayer is talking to God," Eli said.

"If I talk to God, will God talk back to me?" Samuel asked.

"Yes. Your heart will hear Him. But only if you're listening. A long time ago when God talked to His people they heard Him with their ears."

"Doesn't He talk like that to His people anymore?" Samuel asked.

"He probably does. They don't hear Him, though, since they're not listening." Many of God's people had turned away from God. They worshiped statues instead of the Lord God.

Samuel knew what Eli meant about God's

talking to his heart. He knew that feeling of being taken care of when he fell asleep at night. "I wonder," he thought to himself. "If I listen to God, would I hear Him?"

One night Samuel woke up suddenly. Someone was calling him. "Samuel."

"Here I am," Samuel said. He ran to Eli. "Yes Eli. Is there something I can get for you?"

Eli sat up in bed. He looked puzzled. "No, my son. I didn't call you. Go back to sleep."

This happened two more times. Until finally, Eli realized Samuel must be hearing God's voice. "Samuel, I'm not calling you. The Lord is calling you! Answer Him next time by saying, 'Yes Lord, I'm listening.' "

Samuel did this. When God spoke again, Samuel said he was listening. Then God told Samuel what was going to happen. Samuel listened and he trusted God.

15

The next morning, Eli asked Samuel, "So tell me, Samuel. What did the Lord say?"

Samuel swallowed hard. He knew Eli would not like to hear what was going to happen. Samuel also knew that Eli had taught him to always tell the truth. The little boy sighed.

"God told me that your sons have been doing bad things. Because you did not correct them, God will punish your family."

Eli nodded. "He is the Lord. He knows what is right."

This was the first of many times when the Lord spoke to Samuel. God spoke through Samuel. God told the boy things He wanted His people to hear. "Don't worship false gods," Samuel told them. "Love the one God!"

Samuel learned to love the Lord very much. He talked to God. God talked to Samuel. Samuel listened. But often when Samuel told the people what God had said, they did not want to listen.

Before long, a terrible war broke out between the Israelites and their enemies, the Philistines. The Israelites took the box with the Ten Commandments with them into battle. But the Philistines won the battle and captured the Ten Commandments!

This was bad news for everybody, but especially for Eli. He had just heard that his two sons had died in battle. When he heard the news about the Ten Commandments, it was too much for him. He fell over backwards, hit his head on a stone and died.

Now Samuel became the holy leader, the judge, over God's people.

As the years passed Samuel continued to hear God speak. He listened to God and became wiser. Samuel judged the people fairly. Often God told Samuel about things which were going to happen. This meant Samuel could talk to the people as God's prophet, as well as their judge.

Many years went by. One day, Samuel called the people together. "If you want to follow the Lord, you must change. You must pray. Say you are sorry for the times you have not listened. Say you are sorry for worshiping other gods. Thank God for all the good things he has given you. Talk to God and let Him talk to your hearts."

The people prayed. As they were praying, the Philistines found out the Israelites were all in one place. "Now is the time to attack!"

they said to one another. "The Israelites won't be able to fight back while they're praying!"

The Philistines were very wrong. It was because of prayer that God would save the Israelites.

"Samuel! What will we do?" God's people cried out. "Pray to God for us! The Philistines are almost here. They will kill us all!"

Samuel prayed for the people. God answered his prayers. When the Philistines attacked, God filled the sky with thunder.

The thunder boomed around the heads of the Philistines. It roared through the skies! The Philistines screamed! They ran away in fear. The Israelites chased them and won a great battle that day, thanks to God and Samuel's prayers.

Samuel had a family. He and his wife had two sons. As these sons grew older, Samuel tried to teach them about God. They did not want to listen. Still, Samuel let them help him judge the people.

When Samuel judged the people, he always asked God's help. But when his sons judged the problems of the people, they asked for money. Then they always said whatever the rich people wanted to hear.

The people were not fooled. They did not trust Samuel's sons. "How could you let those cheaters judge us?" they complained to Samuel. "When you're gone, there will be no one to lead us well."

"What do you want me to do?" Samuel asked.

The crowd moved up the stairs. "We want a king! We want you to choose a king for us!"

"Yes! A king! We want a king!"

"But God is your King," Samuel told them.

The people did not listen. "All the other countries around us have kings. If we can't trust your sons to judge us fairly, then we want a king!"

Samuel sighed. "I will talk to God about this. Will you listen to what He says?" he asked.

"As long as God says we can have a king!" The people were very stubborn.

Samuel asked God, "What do You want, Lord?"

God said, "You were right to tell the people I should be their King. But since they think they can only follow My laws if they have a king, give them their king. Let them know, though, what it will cost them."

Samuel told the people what God had said. "Are you really sure you want a king? Your children will become his servants. Your sons will have to fight in his army. You will have to give him a share of your crops. God won't help you when you complain about your king!"

The people did not listen. "We want a king! We want a king!"

So Samuel sent them home. And he started waiting for God to show him who should be the first king of Israel.

Before long, God told Samuel, "Tomorrow a stranger will ask you about some lost donkeys. He is the one who will become king. Pour oil on him and bless him."

Samuel waited all day. In the evening he saw a tall, handsome man walking toward the city gates. The man's name was Saul. Saul asked, "Do you know where the holy man Samuel is? I am trying to find my father's lost donkeys. I was hoping he could help me."

Samuel smiled. "I am Samuel. Your donkeys have already been found. I'm on my way to a feast on top of this hill. The people there are worshiping God." Samuel pointed up the hill. "Come join me and you can sit at the head of the table." Saul did not know why Samuel should pay him such an honor. But he said yes and followed Samuel up the hill.

When Saul left the next day, Samuel walked with him to the edge of the city. Then he stopped the big man. "God has a message for you, Saul." Saul's eyes grew big.

Samuel said, "The Lord has chosen you to become the first king of Israel."

Saul gasped. "Me? But I come from the smallest family in the smallest tribe. I'm no one important!"

"You are now," Samuel told him. "Now bow your head and I will bless you in God's name."

Saul bowed his head. Samuel poured oil on Saul. This was a sign that God had chosen Saul and would help him to be a good king.

"Go back to your father so he doesn't worry," Samuel said. He told Saul where he could find his father's donkeys. He told him to wait until he was called to become king.

Saul heard Samuel, but did not really understand.

A short time later Samuel called the people together. "God will show you who your king is," he said. Then, out of all the tribes, God chose Saul's tribe. Out of all the families, God chose Saul's family. Out of all the men, God chose Saul.

"Saul? Who is Saul?" the people cried. "Where's this Saul?"

Samuel asked God. The Lord told him that Saul was hiding between all the baskets.

The people ran and found Saul. They brought him to Samuel. "There is your king!" Samuel pointed.

"Oh, he's so tall and handsome. Yes, he will make a good king! Long live Saul! Long live Saul!"

25

At first Saul was a good king. He listened when Samuel told him what God said. But then, slowly but surely, Saul started doing what he wanted, instead of what God wanted.

He grew proud. "I'm a great king," he often thought. "Tell me I'm a great king," he ordered his servants.

"You are a great king," they told him.

But Samuel warned Saul to be careful. "You should not be so proud of yourself." Saul ignored Samuel's advice.

All this time the Israelites were still fighting wars against their enemies. During one of these battles, Saul did something very bad. He tried to be king without God. He did just what he wanted to instead of what God had told him to do.

Samuel had told Saul, "God wants you to kill every one of these enemies. Destroy all their animals and treasures." Saul had his orders from God. But did he listen? No.

Instead, when Saul saw how rich this enemy tribe was, he stole their animals and treasures for his army. And he chose not to kill their king.

God was sad that Saul had not listened again. So God was sorry He had made Saul

king. He sent Samuel to warn Saul that he had done something very wrong by not doing what God had ordered.

Even then Saul would not listen. Instead, he made excuses. "We thought we could use the animals as sacrifices to God. But it's not really my fault. My army did it. I didn't do it."

Samuel knew Saul was lying. "The Lord says He would rather you had listened to Him than offer animals for sacrifices. Because you've become so proud, He doesn't want you to be the king anymore." Saul knew he had made a terrible mistake.

God sent Samuel to find the man who would become king after Saul. Samuel traveled to Bethlehem. There he visited a man named Jesse. When Samuel met Jesse's sons, he asked God which one would become the new king. "The eldest is very handsome, Lord," Samuel said.

"I don't look at a person's outside beauty," God said. "I look at the heart."

Samuel asked if there were no other sons. Jesse sent for his youngest boy. He was taking care of the sheep. "This is David," Jesse said.

God told Samuel, "This is the one." Samuel poured oil over David's head. This was a sign that God was blessing him in a very special way and that someday he would become king.

At that time, David was just a boy who loved God in his heart very much. In many ways he was just like Samuel had been when he was a boy. They both knew how to pray to God and listen for answers in their hearts.

In the years to come, Samuel learned how wise a choice God had made. David proved how much he trusted God by fighting the giant Goliath. David was so brave, Saul made him the captain of his army.

One time when Saul and David were riding back from a battle side by side, women danced around them and sang, "Saul has killed thousands, but David has killed his tens of thousands!"

This made Saul very angry. He was still king, but ever since Samuel had told him God would choose another king, Saul had felt jealous and troubled. Samuel had warned Saul, but he had not listened. Now it was too late.

Saul's anger turned him into a mean man. As time went by, he could not stop thinking of how jealous he was of David. Nothing Samuel said could change Saul's mind.

Finally, even though David was his best fighter, Saul tried to kill him. So David ran away to Samuel.

"The king thinks I want to take his place. He's wrong," David told Samuel. "I will listen to Saul as long as God wants me to. I was in the throne room when he suddenly picked up his spear and threw it at me! Why Samuel? Why does the king hate me so much?"

Samuel was a very, very old man by this time. He sighed. "You listen to the Lord in your heart, David. This is why God chose you. Someday He will make you king. Saul knows you are special and wants that for himself."

Samuel took David's young hands in his old hands. "You must run away from Saul and keep yourself safe, David. Never forget, though, to ask God what you should do. Listen to His answers and you will stay as special to Him as you were when you were a boy."

David hid from Saul for many years. During this time, Samuel grew so old that he finally died. When Samuel died, he went to heaven.

Samuel was the last judge of Israel. And he was the first prophet for Israel. All his life he had prayed for God's people. While Saul chased David, Samuel prayed for David. God heard Samuel's prayers. After Samuel's death, Saul was killed in battle and David became the greatest king Israel ever had.

All that Samuel had said would happen, did happen. . . because he trusted what he heard God say.

You can find the story of Samuel in the Old
Testament Book of First Samuel, chapters 1-25.